Thrill Rides!
ALL ABOUT ROLLER COASTERS

BY JEFF SAVAGE

MONDO

For information contact:
MONDO Publishing
980 Avenue of the Americas
New York, NY 10018

Visit our website at http://www.mondopub.com

Printed in China
07 08 09 10 11   9 8 7 6 5 4 3 2 1
ISBN 1-59336-727-9 (PB)

Designed by Witz End Design

Library of Congress Cataloging-in-Publication Data

Savage, Jeff, 1961-
    Thrill rides! : all about roller coasters / by Jeff Savage.
       p. cm.
    Includes index.
    ISBN 1-59336-727-9 (pbk.)

1. Roller coasters--History--Juvenile literature. 2. Roller coasters--Design
and construction--Juvenile literature. 3. Roller coasters--United States--
History--Juvenile literature. I. Title.
GV1860.R64S28 2006
688.7--dc22

CONTENTS

INTRODUCTION

Amusement parks have been a popular form of entertainment in the United States for more than a century. A big part of the parks' appeal is the roller coaster: a giant tangle of twists and turns that sends exhilarated and frightened riders flying through the air in rattling coaster cars. By the end of 2005, about 700 roller coasters dotted the U.S. landscape. Thrill-seekers flock to these scream machines so they can be scared half to death. The coaster is not just an American cultural phenomenon, however. More than 328 million people visited amusement parks around the world in 2004. What was the main attraction? You guessed it: roller coasters.

This book will tell you how roller coasters came to be, who designs them, how they are built, how they work, and whether they are safe to ride. You will learn what rides are the tallest, fastest, and most dangerous. You will see how much of a "thrill" your body can withstand, and you can decide whether you want to accept the challenge. Famous aviator Charles Lindbergh once said that riding the famed Cyclone roller coaster at Coney Island in New York was more thrilling than flying an airplane. But as Lindbergh explained, "A certain amount of danger is essential to the quality of life."

CHAPTER 1

Early Roller Coasters

When did this roller coaster madness begin? Historians have found evidence of thrill-seeking Greeks and Native Americans from as far back as one thousand years ago. But the origin of the roller coaster, as we know it, can be traced to fifteenth-century Russia.

In the nineteenth century, people in France rode wheeled roller coaster cars down grooved tracks.

Roller Coasters of Europe

More than five hundred years ago, the townspeople of St. Petersburg, Russia, built large ramps out of wood, some as high as 70 feet (21.3 m), with strong wooden frameworks for support. Then in the winter, snow would fall and cover the ramps, and an attendant would spray water over the snow, turning it to ice. A passenger would climb a steep staircase to the launching platform at the top of the ramp. There a guide would be seated on a slide, which was just a block of ice shaped like a sled that had a seat lined with straw for warmth and comfort. The passenger would sit on the guide's lap, and together they would ride down the icy ramp. Sand was scattered at the bottom of the ramp to slow down the frozen sled at the end of its journey.

To improve comfort, wooden sleds soon replaced the blocks of ice. The townspeople hung different colored lanterns along the ramp so that night sliding would be possible. These popular ice slides became known as Russian Mountains and were major attractions in Russia. Some ramps were huge, stretching several city blocks. Even the Russian empress Catherine the Great (1729-1796) was a big fan of these slides. Many historians believe she was responsible for the invention of the first real "roller coaster" when she had her slide fitted with wheels so that she could ride it year round.

About the turn of the nineteenth century, a Frenchman visiting Russia took a ride on an ice slide, and he was so impressed that he returned to France intent on building a slide there as well. Unfortunately, the ice wouldn't stay frozen in the warmer French climate; changes were needed. Instead of being made of snow and ice, tracks were made of wooden rollers, and the sleds were given runners on the bottoms that enabled the sleds to glide over the rollers.

These rides became a huge hit at public gardens in France. They were called Les Montagnes Russes (The Russian Mountains). Before long, French engineers had improved on the rather slow-moving coaster by designing a grooved track that gave a smoother, faster ride. In 1804 the first wheeled coaster debuted in Paris. It was named **Russian Mountains** after its ancestor. Single-passenger carriages with wheels on the bottom that fit into a groove in the metal track were used. This change helped keep the carriage on the track. However, seat belts had not yet been invented, so passengers often tumbled out of the carriage! Those who did reach the bottom safely faced a long, steep climb back to the top if they wanted another ride.

In 1817 a brand new type of coaster named **Bellevue Mountains** opened near Paris. This coaster had a wide U-shaped track that sent riders hurtling downward and speeding across a straightaway. Momentum then carried the cars back up the other side. To return to their starting point, riders simply took another ride in reverse. That same year a coaster named **Aerial Walks** opened in Paris. For the first time, guardrails lined the tracks to prevent cars and people from hurtling over the sides. On this coaster, two cars holding passengers started on side-by-side tracks. The cars took off at the same time down a steep incline, but then at the bottom of the hill, the tracks curved in opposite directions, meeting again at the starting point. The momentum from the first drop usually provided enough force for the cars to complete the circle; however, occasionally attendants had to push a car the last few feet to the station. A cable system was later installed to pull the cars to the top of the ride.

French engineers designed other interesting coasters. One was built with windmill motors for the cars, while another featured handrails that passengers used to pull themselves up to the starting station. In 1848 a significant innovation was made when an engineer named Monsieur Clavieras designed the first looping track. Sandbags were placed in the cars for the test run, and when the bags did not fall out of the car while it was upside down, passengers began riding. This coaster's strange name was the **Centrifugal Pleasure Railway**.

Clavieras's looping coaster

Mauch Chunk Switchback Railway

The Roller Coaster Comes to America

The roller coaster finally reached the United States in the 1820s— sort of. The Mauch Chunk Railway, in eastern Pennsylvania, was a railroad line used for hauling coal. The cars were loaded with coal and mules at the top of Mount Pisgah, and then they coasted downhill to the canal below, where workers unloaded the coal. The mules then hauled the empty cars back up the track to pick up another load. When a return track was laid, the system became known as the Switchback. So the first passengers on this roller coaster of sorts were mules! It wasn't until some 50 years later that American people discovered the thrill.

By 1870 the coal mines had spread over the mountain, many on flatter ground, and operating the Switchback was no longer profitable. But rather than close down the railway, the citizens of Mauch Chunk decided to offer rides to people for a nickel. While riders enjoyed the beautiful scenery, steam engines pulled the cars to the top of Mount Pisgah. Soon the loop was extended to 18 miles long (29 km), offering a ride that lasted a little over an hour. The exciting finishing run was a 65-mile-per-hour (104.6 kph) rush down the side of Mount Jefferson. In 1873 nearly 35,000 people rode the **Mauch Chunk Switchback Railway**.

The success of the Mauch Chunk ride inspired American designers to build more roller coasters. In 1872, J.G. Taylor of Baltimore, Maryland, was issued one of the first patents for a roller coaster, which was listed at the time as an "Improvement in Inclined Railways." In 1878, Richard Knudsen of Brooklyn, New York, applied for a patent for his "Inclined-Plane Railway." His invention would have featured 30-foot (9.1-m) elevators at each end of two parallel tracks traveling in opposite directions. Riders would have started at the top of the first track, coasted downward to the bottom, then been lifted in their car to the top of the second track. They could then repeat the process. But unfortunately, Knudsen never built his ride.

The "Father of the Gravity Ride"

One inventor who *did* follow through with his plans was LaMarcus A. Thompson. In the late 1800s, Coney Island in Brooklyn, New York, was a tacky beachfront lined with bars and beer gardens. Thompson believed that a roller coaster would improve the area by making it more family-friendly and fun, so he applied for and was issued a patent for his "Roller Coasting Structure." On June 13, 1884, Thompson unveiled his **Gravity Pleasure Switchback Railway**, which consisted of two boarding stations and two straight parallel tracks that stretched 600 feet (182.9 m). The car held 10 passengers and coasted 6 miles (9.7 km) per hour down a gently sloping hill. At the bottom, the riders got out of the car and followed attendants, who pushed the car up to the opposite platform. The passengers then climbed back in and rode along the

second track back to their starting point. It might not sound like a very exciting ride, but for people who had never experienced anything like it, it was a thrill! Riders paid five cents a ride, and the coaster earned about $600 a day—a huge amount of money in those days. Thompson earned money so quickly that he was able to pay for the coaster's entire construction in three weeks.

The success of Thompson's ride sparked competition at Coney Island. Later that year Charles Alcoke of Ohio built his **Serpentine Railway**. The track was designed in the shape of an oval, so cars were sent out over the track and then back again. This continuous loop became known as an "out and back." It was the first design that allowed riders to return to their original starting point without stopping. Six passengers sat in a car shaped like a park bench. The ride was designed this way so the passengers could enjoy the scenery. The cars rolled at 12 miles (19.3 km) per hour—twice as fast as Thompson's coaster. In 1885 a San Franciscan named Phillip Hinckle added his coaster, the **Gravity Pleasure Road**, to the Coney Island landscape. This structure featured a steam-powered chain lift to haul the cars up the first hill. The seats faced forward, so passengers could see where they were going. It didn't take long for Alcoke's and Hinckle's rides to become more popular than Thompson's.

Coney Island's
Serpentine Railway

Not to be outdone, Thompson got to work on an even better coaster. He created an automatic cable grip that could be activated by triggers under the tracks, which prevented cars from accidentally rolling backward. He linked two long cars together, thus creating the first roller coaster train, and added details to the ride, including a tunnel that sent riders into terrifying darkness. Deep in the tunnel, the cars would trigger another recent invention—electric lights. The lights would illuminate images painted on the walls. Riders saw drawings of dragons and devils, paintings of beautiful places, and historical scenes from the Bible. Thompson called his newest ride the **Scenic Railway**.

The first Scenic Railway opened in 1887 on the boardwalk in Atlantic City, New Jersey. Thompson's slogan was "Ride it just for fun," and everyone did. The coaster was an instant success, and Thompson was flooded with orders to build more of these scenic railways. He formed the L.A. Thompson Scenic Railway Company, and by 1888 he had built almost 50 roller coasters in the United States and Europe. Thompson

was widely recognized as the man who popularized using the force of gravity to provide riders with thrills. While it was the scientist and mathematician Sir Isaac Newton who actually explained the laws of gravity, it is LaMarcus Thompson who became known as the "Father of the Gravity Ride."

Roller Coaster Hysteria... and Decline

Roller coaster interest surged near the beginning of the twentieth century, and construction exploded. An inventor named Lina

The Scenic Railway in Rockaway Beach, New York

Beecher built a wild looping coaster in 1888 and sold it to coaster designer Paul Boyton. The ride was called the **Flip-Flap** and was set up at Coney Island. Passengers swooped down a 30-foot (9.1-m) drop and whipped upside down around the loop. The ride lasted 10 seconds. Riders complained of back and neck soreness, however, and the ride soon closed. In 1901 another inventor, Edward Prescott, built a second looping coaster called the **Loop-the-Loop**. Prescott designed his loop as an ellipse, or teardrop shape, not a perfect circle like the **Flip-Flap**. This shape reduced the gravitational force on the passengers, making it a more comfortable ride. But only a single four-passenger car could go through the loop at one time, so the **Loop-the-Loop** was not profitable and soon shut down.

Coney Island's Loop-the-Loop

Coney Island remained a testing ground for new types of roller coasters. **Shoot-the-Chutes** and **Mountain Torrent** were among the first of the modern log rides through water. Then the **Cyclone Bowl** appeared in 1910. These rides were forerunners to what would become the most famous roller coaster ever: the **Cyclone**. Built in 1927, this wooden coaster featured a long, slow climb up an 85-foot (25.9-m) incline at the top of which the car would pause, allowing riders to see the dips and curves of the track below. Designer Vernon Keenan and builder Harry Baker wanted to frighten riders, so they called their creation "The Most Fearsome Coaster Ever Built." The **Cyclone** was so popular that it earned back its more than $100,000 construction costs (equal to over $1 million today) in its first year.

Roller coaster hysteria had spread across the country. In the 1920s, amusement parks sprang up everywhere, and their most popular rides were roller coasters. By this time many people owned cars, so getting to amusement parks was easier than ever. Life was good for most Americans, and the decade was known as "the Roaring Twenties." Such a slogan could also apply to the coaster craze. Designer Harry Guy Traver led the charge by building Cyclones and

other coasters in suburbs across the land. At the height of this golden age, nearly 1,500 wooden coasters were built in the United States. The tallest stood 138 feet high (42.1 m), the fastest traveled 61 miles (98.2 km) per hour, and the designs featured sharp turns, steep drops, and hair-raising dips.

Then in 1929 the Great Depression began. The stock market, in which many Americans had invested their money, collapsed, and most people either lost a great deal of money or went completely broke. They could no longer afford to spend money on things like thrill rides. In 1930 there were between 1,800 and 2,000 amusement parks in the United States, but by 1939 that number had dwindled to just 245. People didn't have extra money

Coney Island's Shoot-the-Chutes

to spend on amusements, so most parks went bankrupt. World War II followed the depression, and the nation's attention was focused elsewhere. Then after the war the emergence of television, which was introduced in 1926 by Scottish inventor John Logie Baird, kept many people in their living rooms. The roller coaster craze had run its course—for now.

But just like the ups and downs of a roller coaster itself, a new interest in these thrill rides would emerge. In 1959 the film producer and director Walt Disney hired a company to build a roller coaster-type ride at his new Disneyland theme park. He called the ride the **Matterhorn Bobsleds**. The coaster's tracks were made of steel, and unlike loud wooden coasters that made loud *clicketyclack* noises, this new one was smooth and quiet. Disney's new coaster started a second wave of roller coaster construction that continues today.

WALT DISNEY: THEME-PARK PIONEER

Walt Disney is one of America's greatest innovators. He was a movie producer, director, voice actor, animator, and cartoonist. He made animated films featuring Mickey Mouse, Donald Duck, Snow White, and Peter Pan—and built the first steel roller coaster.

Walter Elias Disney was born in Chicago, Illinois, in 1901. He grew up with an avid interest in cartooning and in 1923 moved to Hollywood, California. With his brother, Roy, he co-founded the organization now known as The Walt Disney Company. In the late 1940s, Walt began drawing sketches of an amusement park. To help him with his ideas, he hired a group of engineers that he referred to as "Imagineers." The magical park he called Disneyland opened for business on July 17, 1955, in Anaheim, California. One million people visited the park in its first six months, and it has been wildly popular ever since.

To attract even more tourists to the park, Disney hired some engineers to build the world's first steel-tracked roller coaster. It would be called the **Matterhorn Bobsleds** after the Matterhorn mountain on the Switzerland-Italy border, where people rode wooden bobsleds down snowy hills. Disney's famous ride was a 147-foot (44.8-m) replica of the mountain. The peak was built with 2,175 pieces of steel, and the cars looked like bobsleds and rolled on nylon wheels along the tubular-steel track. The track featured sharp twists and turns for maximum thrills. Disney's creation opened in 1959 and greatly increased the popularity of such thrilling and frightening rides.

CHAPTER 2

Roller Design Coaster

LaMarcus Thompson

Roller coasters have dotted the American landscape for more than a century. In spite of their large numbers, these giant structures are not easy to build; coasters require both the skilled work of engineers and the colorful imagination of designers. Civil engineers plan the basic structure, mechanical engineers figure out the mechanics needed to operate the ride, electrical engineers work out the control systems, and designers come up with the look of the coaster, including color, lights, and graphics. It takes a highly talented team to build a thrill ride.

Great American Roller Coaster Companies

There is no school that teaches a person how to design a roller coaster. Great coaster builders come from many backgrounds. For example, the first famous American coaster designer, LaMarcus A. Thompson, was originally a Sunday school teacher from Ohio. Thompson had been inventing things since the age of 12, such as a butter churn for his mother, an oxcart for his father, and riding carts for his friends. As an adult he focused attention on coaster design. His hard work and ingenuity paid off; he received 30 patents for his various innovations.

An engineer named Harry Guy Traver is famous for building coasters that are particularly terrifying. Traver created the **Cyclone**—the famous wooden beast with a spiraling drop and sharp turns. The **Crystal Beach Cyclone** opened in 1927 in Ontario, Canada, and triggered a rush to build similar heart-stopping rides. Traver started out as a schoolteacher but then became a mechanical engineer for the General Electric Company. His coaster career was born when, one day while out sailing, he noticed a flock of sea gulls circling the boat's mast. This image gave him an idea for a new kind of amusement ride. Traver built the Circle Swing, an 80-foot-high (24.4 m) pole with several arms near the top from which cars hung and swung out. As the pole turned, passengers in the cars flew around the pole in the air. The Circle Swing was just the beginning for Traver. He eventually turned his attention to creating bone-rattling roller coasters, but he would recall, "Sea gulls got me into this crackpot business."

Thompson, Traver, and other early inventors formed "companies" to construct their coasters and hired experts to assist them in assembling their designs. One of the most popular companies was the Philadelphia Toboggan Company, which opened in 1904. Started by Henry Auchey and Chester Albright, this company's strength was its team of creative geniuses, who were recognized for improving coaster construction and safety. About fifty years after the company was founded, John Allen took over as president. Allen's biggest achievement was overseeing the construction of the **Racer**, which opened to the public at Kings Island in Cincinnati, Ohio, in 1972, and spawned a new era of ultra-fast coasters.

John Allen's coaster, the Racer

The most famous roller coaster company ever is the Arrow Development Company. In the early 1950s, Ed Morgan and Karl Bacon, at the time machine shop owners in Mountain View, California, were asked by Walt Disney to build the **Matterhorn Bobsleds**. Morgan and Bacon had never built a roller coaster before and didn't feel the need to conform to the standards of the day. Using new technology and materials, they came up with tubular steel tracks and lightweight fiberglass cars on nylon wheels. It was a revolution in roller coaster construction.

In 1978 the company moved its headquarters to Utah and changed its name to Arrow Dynamics. Ronald V. Toomer assumed control of the company. Toomer had worked as an engineer for the United States space program, although this didn't help him with the design of roller coasters nearly as much as did the years he spent working on hot-rod cars. Other Arrow employees have similar stories. For example, as a kid, Kent Seko enjoyed riding roller coasters, but he never considered building them. He wanted to be an architect and build buildings. But then a friend of his who worked at Arrow Dynamics talked Seko into applying for a job with the company. Seko was hired as a beginning draftsman, and in the decade that followed, he learned enough about how coasters work to join the design team and became an outstanding designer.

The Idea

Every hill, dip, and curve of a roller coaster track is carefully crafted to scare riders—but safely, of course! How do designers do this? First, they start with an idea. Master designer Stan Checketts scribbles many of his coaster designs on paper napkins. One drawing he made came from playing with his children. "It might sound wild, but the concept actually evolved from tossing my nine children in the air when they were little kids," Checketts said. "I used to think, 'There has to be a way to do this on a grander scale.'" The result? Checketts created **Power Tower**, a 300-foot (91.4 m) superstructure at Cedar Point, in Sandusky, Ohio. The coaster blasts riders straight up or straight down at a breathtaking speed of over 50 miles (80.5 km) per hour. Other designers may prefer to use sketchpads instead of napkins, but the process always begins the same way: a drawing of an idea.

Stan Checketts' Power Tower blasts riders straight up — and then down.

The Location

As the designers get their basic concept down on paper, they must consider the location of the actual structure. They might have an area the size of a football stadium to work with, or they might have to squeeze their design onto a tiny lot. Designers must constantly make adjustments to their design. For example, there may be a large tree or rock on the site that requires the coaster to make a dip or sharp turn. Once the basics are figured out, designers then turn to a computer for help. Computers are used to calculate the speeds, gravitational forces (G-forces), and vibration levels generated by a coaster's slopes and curves. If the forces are too great, adjustments are made. This is the same kind of technology used to build rockets.

The Shape

The shape of a coaster's track can range from straightforward to complex and full of turns and twists. There are a variety of tricks a designer can use to give the rider extra thrills and chills. The first corkscrew-shaped coaster, which has a series of loops that take your breath away, opened in 1975 at Knott's Berry Farm in Buena Park, California. Nearby, the **Viper** at Six Flags Magic Mountain in Valencia turns passengers upside down seven times. The **Loch Ness Monster** at Busch Gardens in Williamsburg, Virginia, features a string of vertical loops and whipsaw turns that snap riders around in different directions. The **ArrowBatic** weaves in and out of itself and therefore is able to sit on a smaller area of land. It has several loops and corkscrews and a death-defying vertical drop. The **Magnum XL-200**, built in 1989 for the Cedar Point amusement park in Sandusky, Ohio, was the first coaster to carry its passengers higher than 200 feet (61 m). A coaster reaching such a height became known as a hypercoaster. After its initial climb, the car hurtles down 19 stories, making riders think they are about to crash to Earth.

The first hypercoaster,
the Magnum XL-200

STAN CHECKETTS: MASTER DESIGNER

Stan Checketts wasn't always a master roller coaster designer. For 35 years he worked as a cabinetmaker. But the whole time, Checketts had a secret dream to design a machine that would send people flying through the air. Checketts was a thrill seeker. He liked snowmobiling at high speeds, jumping out of airplanes, and diving to the bottom of the ocean. Finally Checketts decided to act on his dream. First he designed a trampoline for children. Not satisfied, he built a bungee tower, in which riders jumped from the top and fell until a bungee cord stopped their fall.

Soon Checketts was learning about roller coaster technology and started a company now called S&S Power, Inc., in his hometown of Logan, Utah. Today Checketts has a staff of about 60 people. The company designs and builds thrill rides for amusement parks everywhere. One of the company's most popular rides is the **Stratosphere Big Shot** in Las Vegas, Nevada. Riders are launched straight up in their seats to a height of 160 feet (48.8 m) in 2.5 seconds and then dropped at the same speed of 45 miles (72.4 km) per hour.

Checketts' compressed air-powered roller coaster in Japan is among the world's fastest—it goes from zero to 107 miles (172.2 km) per hour in two seconds. **Swat** at Six Flags AstroWorld in Houston, Texas, pushes passengers down 100 feet (30.5 m) toward the ground as if they are being smacked by a giant fly swatter. "We do amazing things with air," Checketts says. Checketts has built 115 tower rides, 150 children's rides, and 3 pure coasters in 24 countries around the world. "I'm a high-thrill person," he says. "My job is a blast—literally."

CHAPTER 3

Types of Roller Coasters

Roller coasters come in many shapes and sizes. But all coasters can be separated into two main groups: those that are made of wood and those made of steel. When a coaster is described as being made of wood or steel, this doesn't refer to the track supports—the giant structures under the tracks—but rather to the material the tracks themselves are made of. Wooden coasters feature tracks built with wood planks, while steel coasters have rails made of steel pipes. In fact, some steel coasters are supported by wooden beams, and some wooden coasters are propped up with steel poles.

Classic and Beloved Woodies

Wooden coasters are affectionately known as "woodies." These were the first wave of American coasters built in the first half of the twentieth century. Nearly all woodies feature a starting lift hill, on which cars are pulled to the top by a chain or cable, creating that familiar clicketyclack sound. Once at the top, the cars are released, and riders are sent speeding down. The direction they go depends on whether they are riding an out-and-back coaster or a twister coaster. An out-and-back coaster goes out from the station, turns, and comes

back. The track has some curves but is known mainly for its dips and rises. A twister coaster winds around itself in all directions and features swooping turns mixed with death-defying drops. Wooden coasters are still being built today, because many riders prefer the bone-rattling sensation of a woodie—caused by the wheels against the rails on the wooden track—to the smoother feel of steel.

The most famous woodie still operating today is the **Cyclone** at Coney Island. This coaster uses iron girders to support its wooden track and has a twister design that offers riders nine drops and six curves. It reaches a top speed of 60 miles (96.5 km) per hour. Though it stands just 85 feet tall (25.9 m)—small compared to today's mammoth coasters, which can tower over 400 feet tall (122 m)—it still packs a powerful punch. The original **Cyclone** spawned many imitations that are still in operation, including coasters at Six Flags Over Georgia, Six Flags New England, and Six Flags Magic Mountain in Southern California.

The Cyclone at Coney Island

Just as Coney Island's Cyclone inspired many wooden imitations, the **Racer** at Paramount's Kings Island in Cincinnati, Ohio, triggered the second golden age of wooden coasters. The **Racer** opened in 1972 with a pair of sleek out-and-back coasters that run on parallel tracks in opposite directions. **Rebel Yell** at Paramount's Kings Dominion in Virginia and **Thunder Road** at Paramount's Carowinds in North Carolina are examples of similar racers that followed. But the father of all racers is the structure at Pennsylvania's Kennywood, simply known as **Racer**. Built in 1927, its parallel tracks are so close that riders in opposite cars are nearly elbow to elbow. Twisters generally are less predictable than out-and-back coasters, but this doesn't mean out-and-backs don't provide thrills. Taking only one ride on the **Giant Dipper** in Santa Cruz, California, proves just that. This is one of the few boardwalk coasters left in the world, and though it stands just 70 feet (21.3 m) high, the **Giant Dipper's** many dips and turns lift riders out of their seats, giving the more than 50 million people who have ridden it since its opening in 1924 plenty of thrills.

Two of the most powerful woodies in operation today are **Colossus** and **The Beast**. When the 125-foot-tall (38.1-m) **Colossus** opened in 1978 at Six Flags Magic Mountain in Valencia, California, it was the largest wooden coaster in the world. This double track out-and-back style coaster features a 115-foot (35-m) first drop and provides riders with over three minutes of breathtaking excitement. Then, a year after **Colossus** came to life, **The Beast** was born. Looming in the woods at Paramount's Kings Island, it became the world's tallest and fastest woodie, and with 7,400 feet (2,255.5 m) of track, it's still the longest. **The Beast's** initial climb stretches 135 feet (41.2 m), after which the cars hurtle down at 65 miles (104.6 km) per hour through 35 acres (14.2 hectares) of densely wooded terrain. **Colossus** and **The Beast** were topped in the year 2000 by the only "hyperwoodie" [one over 200 feet (61 m) tall] in the world. **Son of Beast**, also located at Kings Island, stands 218 feet tall (66.4 m), casting a shadow over its "father," **The Beast**. **Son of Beast** is the only looping woodie in existence, and it gives riders the thrill of roaring down the track at nearly 80 miles (128.7 km) per hour and then spinning through its 118-foot-tall (36-m) loop.

Son of Beast at Kings Island is a "hyperwoodie."

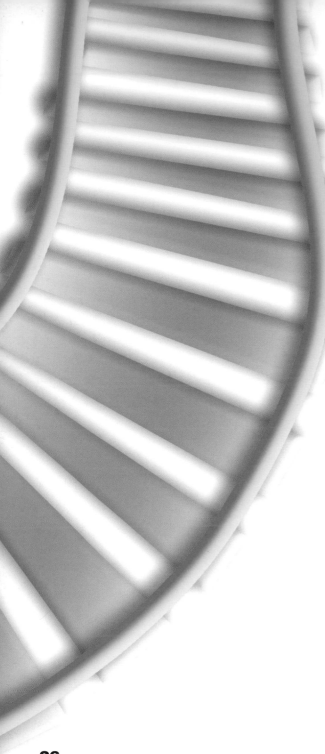

Super Steel Coasters

Steel coasters generally are bigger, faster, and more modern than their wooden counterparts. The **Matterhorn Bobsleds** at Disneyland ignited, in 1959, a steel coaster explosion that continues today. Steel coasters offer a smoother and quieter ride because the cars' wheels run along slick steel piping. Builders can bend and stretch the steel into almost any shape. There are out-and-back steel coasters, twister steel coasters, and other styles. The sky's the limit for steel coaster designs.

Steel coasters are able to send passengers in all directions because steel can be bent in endless ways. Some coasters carry riders underground and through tunnels where they can enjoy lights, images, and other special effects that make a ride more thrilling. Starry lights, for instance, can give the illusion that the car is moving faster than it actually is. The **Adventure Express** at Kings Island pretends to be a runaway mine train, crossing through streams and plunging down a dark mine shaft. Not being able to see where they are going can also make a ride scarier for riders. The **Road Runner Express** in San Antonio, Texas, shows images of the cartoon characters Road Runner and Wile E. Coyote on the walls of the dark tunnels the cars speed through. An indoor ride equipped with special effects is also known as a dark ride.

The cars on steel coasters do not always sit on the tracks. To provide riders with an extra thrill, some cars hang below the tracks in what are called suspended coasters. The first modern one was **The Bat**, which opened in 1981 at Kings Island. Unfortunately, **The Bat** was not in flight for long. Frequent mechanical problems kept it closed much of the time, and about three years later it was torn down. But designers did not abandon the suspended-car concept. In 1984 **Big Bad Wolf** opened at Busch Gardens in Williamsburg, Virginia, featuring cars that swung, swayed, and gave riders the feeling of flying through the air.

Big Bad Wolf at Busch Gardens is a suspended coaster.

Hypercoasters and Gigacoasters

The term *hypercoaster* was coined in 1989 to describe the world's first roller coaster featuring a hill or drop of 200 feet (61 m) or more. That's over 20 stories high! The birthplace of the first hypercoaster, the **Magnum XL-200**, was Cedar Point in Sandusky, Ohio. Arrow Dynamics, the company that had made the first steel coaster 30 years earlier, designed this hypercoaster that features a vertical drop of 200 feet. Five years after **Magnum XL-200** opened, the **Pepsi Max Big One** in Blackpool, England, surpassed it. This coaster lifts riders 213 feet (64.9 m) into the air and offers a beautiful view of the Irish Sea before plunging them down at a speed of 74 miles (119.1 km) per hour.

Over the past 15 years, new steel hypercoasters have sprouted up everywhere. **Raging Bull** at Six Flags Great America in Gurnee, Illinois, and **Apollo's Chariot** at Busch Gardens in Williamsburg, Virginia, feature high seats that allow riders' feet to hang down and sway in the air, with just a lap bar safely holding riders in place. In 2001, Six Flags Great Adventure in Jackson, New Jersey, introduced **Nitro**, an out-and-back hypercoaster with an initial drop of 230 feet (70 m) and seven additional short and fast hills, called camelbacks. **Goliath**, at Six Flags Magic Mountain, stands 235 feet tall (71.6 m), but its first drop is an even longer 255 feet (77.7 m) because the track drops into an underground tunnel.

Once 200-foot hypercoasters became commonplace at parks throughout the country, designers took coasters to the next level, pushing past the 300-foot (91.4-m) mark. These massive structures are the "gigacoasters." Eleven years after Cedar Point opened the first hypercoaster, it made history again by introducing the world's first gigacoaster: **Millennium Force**. This ride towers 310 feet (94.5 m) above ground, and its first drop of 300 feet (91.4 m) is an almost impossibly steep 80 degrees. (A 90-degree drop would be straight down!) Riders plummet about 30 stories toward Earth at 93 miles (149.6 km) per hour and then are swept up and away into a flurry of twists and turns.

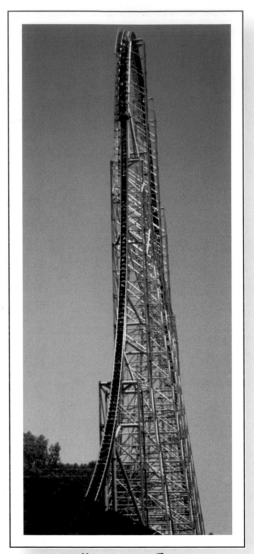

Millennium Force at Cedar Point features a 300-foot initial drop.

Free-Fall Rides

A new challenge in thrill rides was a 90-degree drop. In 1998 **Power Tower** opened at Cedar Point, featuring four 240-foot-tall (73.2-m) steel towers, with outward-facing seats attached to the towers. Seats on two of the towers blast riders up to the top in three seconds going about 60 miles (96.5 km) per hour. Seats on the other two towers blast riders down at the same breakneck speed. Because the ride has four towers, it can accommodate about 1,700 passengers an hour. **Thrill Shot** at Six Flags Magic Mountain and **ErUPtion** at Frontier City outside Oklahoma City feature similar free-fall rides.

Before **Power Tower**, however, thrill seekers had already been experiencing the free-fall sensation for nearly a year. **Superman The Escape** opened at Magic Mountain in 1997, and although it was not technically a straight-up-and-down track, it did offer riders a "weightless" experience. On this L-shaped ride, passengers rocket out of the station and quickly reach a top speed of 100 miles (160.9 km) per hour on their way up a 41-story tower measuring 415 feet (126.5 m) in height. Upon reaching the top, the cars pause briefly and then plummet back the way they came. This ride was not only the tallest and fastest free-fall coaster when it opened, but it was also the first reverse free-fall, where riders fall backward. Because of this path, **Superman The Escape** is also called a shuttle coaster. A shuttle coaster doesn't form a complete circuit, but rather the cars go in one direction on the track, stop, and repeat the course in the opposite direction, with cars and riders moving backward this time.

Superman The Escape's claim to fame didn't last long, of course. In 2003, passengers aboard **Top Thrill Dragster** at Cedar Point were able to go higher and faster than ever before. This coaster launches riders forward, reaching a speed of 120 miles (193.1 km) per hour in four seconds. Then cars rocket straight up a 420-foot-high (128-m) hill and free fall back down at the same incredible speed. The drop over the hill on **Top Thrill Dragster** gives passengers maximum airtime, which is the time riders feel as if they are suspended in air with their bodies lifted up out of their seats.

Top Thrill Dragster at Cedar Point

Other Types of Roller Coasters

Another coaster variation is the inverted coaster, which has cars that run below the tracks. But unlike suspended coasters, the cars do not hang and sway, though passengers are seated with their legs dangling, much like a chair ski lift. Six Flags Great America in Gurnee, Illinois, introduced the first inverted roller coaster in 1992 with **Batman The Ride**. Other Batman rides soon began popping up at other amusement parks.

A variation of the inverted coaster is the floorless coaster, where riders sit as they do for an inverted coaster with legs dangling, but instead of the cars remaining beneath the track, they are able to roll around the track with the force of the momentum. The first floorless coaster, called **Medusa**, debuted in 1999 at Six Flags Great Adventure in Jackson, New Jersey. Designed by Bolliger & Mabillard, this demon zooms through seven inversions at speeds of over 60 miles (96.5 km) per hour. Riders of this coaster are barely in their seats for the entire ride.

The first stand-up coaster, **King Cobra** at Kings Island, Ohio, opened in 1984, and featured a 66-foot-high (20.1-m) vertical loop. In 1998, **Riddler's Revenge**, a stand-up coaster that's about double the size of **King Cobra**, opened at Six Flags Magic Mountain. This ride features a 124-foot (37.8-m) loop and a huge 250-foot (76.2-m) spiral.

Batman The Ride is an inverted coaster.

Face/Off in Paramount's Kings
Island is a floorless coaster.

Roller Coaster Construction

How are these giant structures assembled? This feat is the job of the manufacturing, or fabrications, department. After designers draw up the plans, called blueprints, a team of builders carefully follows the plans. It can take a year or more to put up a roller coaster. Sometimes builders are lifted 300 feet (91.4 m) or higher in cranes to work on the structure and may stay up there all day. People who are scared of heights need not apply.

A massive amount of material is needed to build a roller coaster. In 1993, for example, The Great Escape amusement park in Lake George, New York, acquired a vintage wooden coaster called the **Comet**. This ride was trucked to the park in pieces and then reassembled. Its construction required 1,632 gallons (6,177 liters) of paint, 1,200 yards (1,097.3 m) of concrete, 253,225 board feet (77,183 m) of lumber, and 56,930 boards. It took about a year and cost $3.5 million to complete the reassembly.

A roller coaster is much more than just cars on a track. First, tons of scaffolding, or supporting framework, are needed to hold up the track. Scaffolding can consist of large wooden planks or steel beams, or a combination of the two. Next, builders must construct the mechanics of the ride. For instance, the lift hill is made up of the track itself, the rolling chain lift beneath it, and all the components under the car. Chain dogs are hooks on the cars that attach to the chain lift and are used to pull the car up the lift hill. Ratchets are toothed steel bars on the track that cause a clack, clack, clack sound. If the car accidentally starts to roll backward, ratchet dogs fastened

Workers on a coaster at Six Flags in California

to the car catch the ratchet and stop the car. Pneumatic brakes (brakes powered by air pressure) are installed on the track. A computer controls the overall system, but the ride operator also can control the brakes if necessary in an emergency. Coaster cars have three types of wheels:

• Road wheels sit on top of the track rail and carry the car.

• Upstop wheels fit under the rail and prevent the car from flying off the track. They are also called under-friction or underside wheels.

• Guide wheels run along the side of the rail and keep the car from sliding sideways off the track.

Safety restraint devices, such as seat belts and over-the-shoulder safety harnesses, are standard equipment on coasters.

Some roller coasters are built at a factory and then taken apart and shipped in pieces to the amusement park where they are reassembled—a slow and painstaking process. For example, in August 2000, the **Thrust Air 2000**, built in Logan, Utah, was taken apart and shipped in sections to its new home at Paramount's Kings Dominion in Doswell, Virginia. It took more than 60 trucks traveling a total of 132,000 miles (212,428 km) to haul the materials. Then builders had to spend more than three months reassembling the coaster. Once it was put back

together, the new coaster was tested with 150-pound (68.1-kg) sandbags in the seats instead of real passengers. Next, park workers volunteered to ride. Designer Stan Checketts test-rode it several times. Finally, the **HyperSonic XLC**, as it was renamed, opened for business in March 2001. The entire process took about eight months.

Kingda Ka under construction in 2005

A once-standard roller coaster component that is no longer necessary is the lift hill and its supporting chain gear. Many new coasters still use this system, but now it's merely one of several options. The future of roller coaster motion involves magnets and air. A linear induction motor (LIM) uses high-powered magnetic force like a slingshot to propel coasters through a launch track. Metal fins are attached along the sides of the cars, and several LIMs are placed in the track in the launch area. Electricity creates a magnetic force that attracts metal, including the metal fins, and this force pulls the cars along the track. In 1996 **Flight of Fear** became the first coaster powered by a linear induction motor. Other coasters such as **Mr. Freeze**, **Poltergeist**, and **Volcano**, **The Blast Coaster** soon followed.

In 1997 a second magnetic technology emerged, using a linear synchronous (SIN-kruh-nus) motor (LSM). Like LIMs, LSMs use high-powered magnetic force. In this case, however, the magnetic force is used differently. A basic magnetic law,

A worker inspects the Geauga Lake coaster in Ohio

known as the "law of magnetism," states that two opposite poles, or ends, of a magnet attract. Another law states that two like poles of a magnet repel. On LSM cars, magnets are attached underneath, and LSMs are in the track. Electricity creates a magnetic force that pulls the car over the LSMs by attraction and then repels the magnets on the car, making it go faster. **Superman The Escape** at Six Flags Magic Mountain used an LSM to become the first coaster to send riders soaring 100 miles (161 km) per hour. Finally, compressed air technology was introduced in 2001 with the **HyperSonic XLC** (Extreme Launch Coaster) in Virginia. This coaster was the first to have cars that are launched by air.

THE MAKING OF THE BEAST

The design and construction of **The Beast** at Paramount's Kings Island, Ohio, was a three-year project that cost $3.8 million and involved hundreds of people. The famous woodie was designed by engineer and park director Charles Dinn, but he had plenty of help. Consultants from the Philadelphia Toboggan Company, the oldest existing roller coaster manufacturing company in the world, assisted his in-house team of experts. Together they combined features from other popular rides to create **The Beast**—a magnificent structure that curves and dips along 35 acres (14.2 hectares) of rolling woodland to form the longest wooden track in the world.

The making of **The Beast** required the following:

- 4,300 hours of design time
- 87,000 hours of construction time
- 2,432 square yards (2,033.2 sq m) of poured concrete, enough to pave about a 3.5-mile (5.6-km) stretch of two-lane road
- 650,000 board feet (198,120 m) of redwood lumber
- 37,500 pounds (17,025 kg) of nails
- 82,480 bolts

Four managers, 6 engineers, 17 technicians, and 53 construction workers watched the coaster's first run on April 14, 1979. **The Beast** has been thrilling riders ever since.

CHAPTER 4

Roller Coaster Science

As a roller coaster rises, drops, curves, and dips along the track, many scientific forces are at work.

Forms of Energy

One of the most important factors in the working of a roller coaster is energy. A roller coaster has two forms of energy: potential energy and kinetic (kih-NET-ik) energy. Potential energy, or stored energy, is the amount of energy a coaster has based on its height above the ground. The higher a coaster is, the more potential energy it has. Potential energy is somewhat like fuel. The more fuel a coaster has, the farther it can travel. Kinetic energy, or energy in motion, is the amount of energy a coaster is using. This is determined by the speed of the coaster. The faster a coaster is traveling, the more kinetic energy it has. The combined potential and kinetic energy of a roller coaster is its total energy. While the amount of total energy a coaster has never changes, the amount of each specific form of energy does.

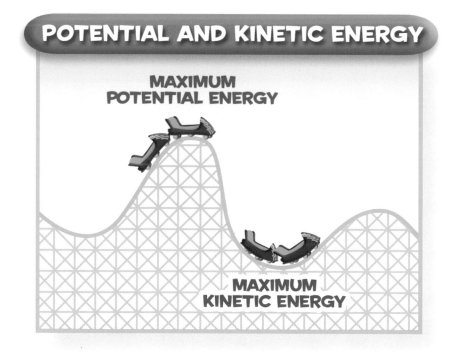

POTENTIAL AND KINETIC ENERGY

MAXIMUM POTENTIAL ENERGY

MAXIMUM KINETIC ENERGY

A roller coaster's highest point determines the total amount of energy it has. It will never have more energy than it has at that point. At the top of the first lift hill, when the coaster is stopped for an instant, it has the most potential energy and zero kinetic energy. The coaster will not be able to go any higher. Designers know that the top of the first lift hill must be as high or higher than any other hill on the track. As the coaster rolls down the first hill, potential energy turns into kinetic energy. The farther the coaster goes down the hill, the less potential energy it has, but the more kinetic energy it gains. The result is measured as speed. The coaster travels fastest at the bottom of the hill because all the potential energy has turned into kinetic energy by that point. Then, as the coaster begins to roll up the next hill, potential energy increases and kinetic energy decreases.

Gravitational Force

The force that causes a coaster to speed down a hill is gravity, which is the force pulling everything toward Earth's surface. Gravitational force is commonly called "G-force." Normal Earth gravity has a G-force of 1, so a person just standing feels 1 G, and roller coaster riders feel a force of 1 G when the coaster is not moving. G-forces greater than 1 make a person feel heavier, for example, as the coaster speeds quickly upward. A force of 3 G's makes people feel three times as heavy as they really are. Astronauts at liftoff experience about 3 G's. For example, a person weighing 100 pounds (45.4 kg) who is experiencing 2.5 G's will feel as if he or she weighs 250 pounds (113.4 kg). When a roller coaster is going uphill, it is moving against gravity, so the gravitational pull is stronger. For this reason, roller coaster riders feel heavier when the coaster accelerates, or speeds, uphill. Most roller coasters do not operate beyond 4 G's. People get nosebleeds at about 6 G's and can become unconscious at about 7 G's.

At the top of a coaster's loop, riders may feel weightless.

G-forces of less than 1 make a person feel lighter. When a roller coaster is going downhill, it is moving with gravity, so the gravitational pull is less. This is why roller coaster riders feel lighter when the coaster accelerates downhill. When a coaster car reaches the top of a hill, just as it is about to start back down, riders may feel 0 G's, or weightless. This feeling is called airtime—a feeling of not weighing anything that thrills most riders. Some rides produce five to six seconds of straight airtime.

Other Roller Coaster Forces

Other forces that control a roller coaster include friction and drag. The law of inertia (in-ER-sha) states that an object in motion will stay in motion unless another force acts on it. For instance, if there were no forces acting on it, a roller coaster car going uphill would continue to climb at the same rate of speed forever. However, there are several forces that act on a coaster to prevent this from happening. The first is the force of gravity. Another is the direction of the track. The wheels of a coaster car are locked onto the track, so when the track changes direction, the coaster must turn and follow that path. This turning results in friction, which is caused by two objects rubbing together. This friction between the track and the wheels slowly drains the coaster of its kinetic energy. Another force, drag, is caused by air resistance. The air pushes against the coaster, slowing it down.

Two other forces affect roller coaster riders. When a roller coaster goes through a turn or a loop, centripetal (sen-TRIP-uh-tul) force (the force that causes an object to move inward) pushes the rider inward around a curve. *Centripetal* means "center-seeking." Centripetal force pushes the rider toward the center of the curve as the coaster goes around the turn. However, when a coaster is headed along a straight line but then swerves around a turn, the rider's body wants to continue in a straight line. As a result, the rider is pushed toward the outer side of the car at the same time the centripetal force is pushing the rider inward toward the center of the turn. The force exerted by the rider on the outer side of the car as it goes through the turn is centrifugal (sen-TRIF-uh-gul) force.

Sir Isaac Newton's third law of motion states that for every action there is an equal and opposite reaction. Centripetal and centrifugal forces are equal and opposite reactions. When a coaster car turns and the rider is forced to turn with it, that pushing force is centripetal force. The amount of force the rider then has on the side of the car is centrifugal force and is equal to the amount of centripetal force. In other words, the force acting on the rider is centripetal force, while the opposite force by the rider is centrifugal force.

Passengers being pushed to the outer side of a coaster car by centrifugal force

CHAPTER 5

Who Likes Roller Coasters?

Imagine you are locked in your seat at the station, about to ride a horrific-looking, monster roller coaster. As the coaster car lurches forward, you nervously say, "Here we go," as your heart pounds. The car slowly climbs the first lift hill, and you start to sweat—you know what's coming. Then there's a split second at the top of the hill when the car pauses, before…whoosh!…it begins its steep drop. You let out your first scream. The car zooms through turns, lifts, and loops. Your heart pounds faster. Your eyes water. You are lightheaded, even dizzy. Your stomach is squashed by G-forces. Finally you return to the station safely and catch your breath. "Let's go again," you say, out of breath from what just happened.

Why do some people love roller coasters? Why do others avoid them? Riding a coaster is scary for everyone, which means some people must like being scared, while others don't. When the human brain senses danger, a biological reaction occurs. A part of the brain called the amygdala (uh-MIG-duh-luh) sends out distress signals to the rest of the body, and in response a heightened sense of awareness takes over.

Roller coaster riders enjoy the thrill.

Endorphins (en-DOR-finz), chemicals that are naturally released in the brain during times of stress and that give relief from pain, are released. These natural painkillers make a person feel good, which is why being scared on a roller coaster can actually feel pleasant. Still, some people may avoid coasters because of a fear of heights, a sense of loss of control, or an illogical fear that the coaster is doomed to crash.

True coaster fans use certain tricks to enhance sensations. As the coaster goes over a hill, they lift their feet off the floor of the car and look up in order to sharpen the feeling of falling through the air. As the coaster goes through a loop, they might look to the side to make themselves feel sick. Or, at another point during the ride, they might look backward to make themselves dizzy. Although these feelings are extremely unpleasant to the ordinary person, many roller coaster fans are thrilled by and seek out these same feelings.

More Thrills to Come

What do coaster fans have to look forward to in the future? Plenty. A coaster boom is in full force, and modern technology has catapulted coasters into the twenty-first century. Loopy coasters like **Dragon Kahn** in Spain and **Monte Makaya** in Brazil flip riders upside down eight times. Stand-up coasters, which were all the rage just a few years ago, have led to flying coasters, in which passengers ride lying down like a superhero soaring through the air. Coasters are getting bigger and faster than ever. Six Flags Great Adventure in New Jersey introduced **Kingda Ka**, the world's tallest and fastest coaster in 2005. The ride's hydraulic launch hurtles passengers at the breathtaking speed of 128 miles (206 km) per hour as they shoot 456 feet (139 m) into the air.

Kingda Ka at Six Flags in New Jersey

A Risky Ride?

But is the thrill worth it? Are roller coasters dangerous? They might seem risky, but coasters are carefully designed to be safe as well as scary. If riders often got injured on a specific coaster, no one would ever want to ride it again, and the coaster would close down. In fact, roller coasters are safer than riding on a bicycle or in a car. Coaster operators keep the number of injuries low by posting height, weight, and age limits. These are based on the ride's force—the smaller the person, the less G-force he or she can take. Safety devices include lap bars and over-the-shoulder safety restraints, which hold riders in place. A study in 2003 by the American Association of Neurological Surgeons concluded that gravitational forces on roller coasters are well within levels thought to be safe. But while roller coasters are built to safely scare riders, a ride's scare factor is what makes people enjoy the ride and come back again and again. Therefore, coaster designers try to make each ride *feel* unsafe, even though it is completely safe.

ANTHONY "COASTER TONY" REYNOLDS

On August 5, 2005, Anthony Reynolds climbed aboard **Boulder Dash** at Lake Compounce in Bristol, Connecticut, and rode the woodie's dips and curves as it rolled along the side of a mountain. As Reynolds returned to the station, he was greeted with handshakes and camera flashes. Why? Reynolds had ridden **Boulder Dash** for the 5,000th time. Known as "Coaster Tony," Reynolds had been coming from his home in nearby western Massachusetts regularly on Fridays and Sundays since **Boulder Dash** opened five years earlier. Coaster Tony also has visited every major theme park in America and has ridden over 500 roller coasters. "Wood coasters give a different experience every time you ride," says Coaster Tony, "and there is no better thrill than **Boulder Dash** at Lake Compounce."

Tony Reynolds riding Boulder Dash

CONCLUSION

The roller coaster's history is a long and colorful one. So many incredible coaster innovations have been made over the years that the old expression "The sky's the limit" seems truly to apply to the future of roller coasters! Who knows what the twenty-first century will bring.

Are you among the millions of people who love experiencing the death-defying thrills of roller coasters, or do you prefer to keep your feet firmly on the ground? If you are a coaster fan, the charts that begin on page 44 can give you some ideas about which roller coasters you might want to visit and ride. But beware! If you choose to climb aboard one of these incredible wooden or metal machines, be prepared for the ride of your life!

THE FASTEST ROLLER COASTERS IN THE UNITED STATES

SPEED IN MILES PER HOUR

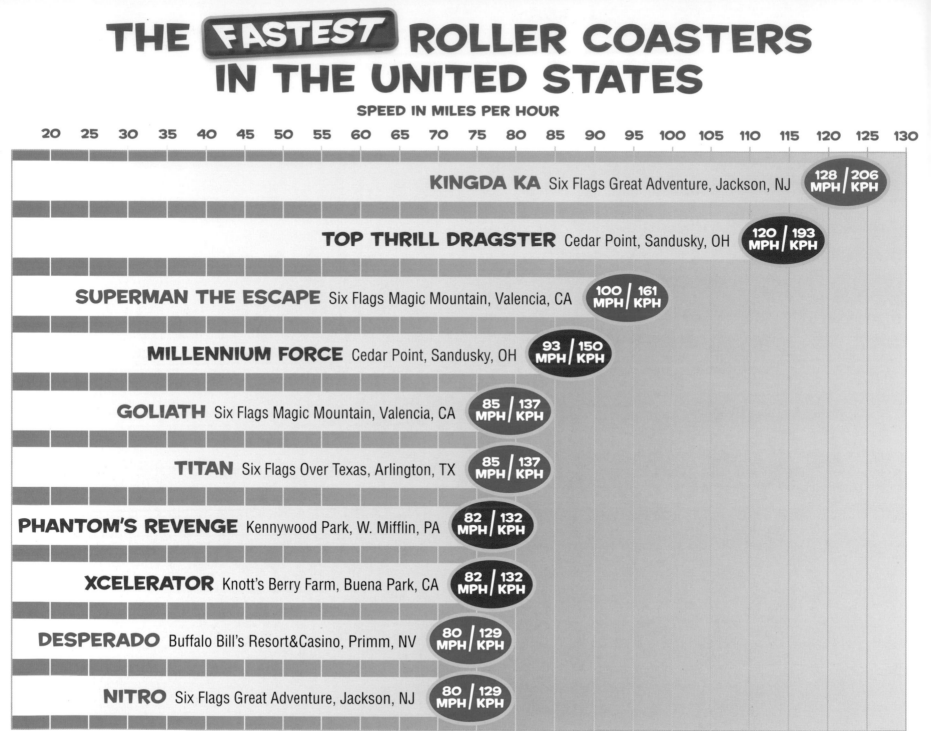

| | 20 | 25 | 30 | 35 | 40 | 45 | 50 | 55 | 60 | 65 | 70 | 75 | 80 | 85 | 90 | 95 | 100 | 105 | 110 | 115 | 120 | 125 | 130 |

KINGDA KA Six Flags Great Adventure, Jackson, NJ — 128 MPH / 206 KPH

TOP THRILL DRAGSTER Cedar Point, Sandusky, OH — 120 MPH / 193 KPH

SUPERMAN THE ESCAPE Six Flags Magic Mountain, Valencia, CA — 100 MPH / 161 KPH

MILLENNIUM FORCE Cedar Point, Sandusky, OH — 93 MPH / 150 KPH

GOLIATH Six Flags Magic Mountain, Valencia, CA — 85 MPH / 137 KPH

TITAN Six Flags Over Texas, Arlington, TX — 85 MPH / 137 KPH

PHANTOM'S REVENGE Kennywood Park, W. Mifflin, PA — 82 MPH / 132 KPH

XCELERATOR Knott's Berry Farm, Buena Park, CA — 82 MPH / 132 KPH

DESPERADO Buffalo Bill's Resort&Casino, Primm, NV — 80 MPH / 129 KPH

NITRO Six Flags Great Adventure, Jackson, NJ — 80 MPH / 129 KPH

THE TALLEST ROLLER COASTERS IN THE UNITED STATES

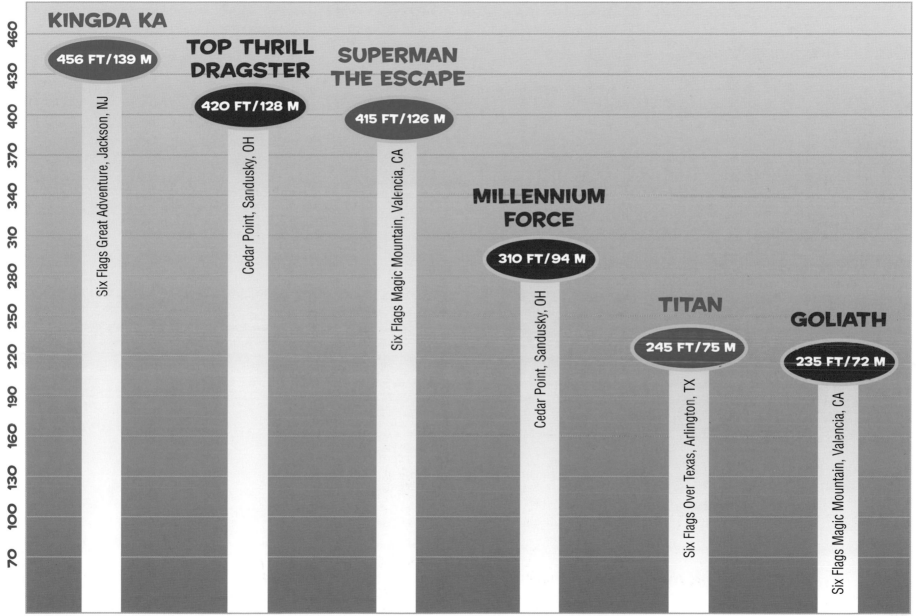

HEIGHT IN FEET

KINGDA KA
456 FT/139 M
Six Flags Great Adventure, Jackson, NJ

TOP THRILL DRAGSTER
420 FT/128 M
Cedar Point, Sandusky, OH

SUPERMAN THE ESCAPE
415 FT/126 M
Six Flags Magic Mountain, Valencia, CA

MILLENNIUM FORCE
310 FT/94 M
Cedar Point, Sandusky, OH

TITAN
245 FT/75 M
Six Flags Over Texas, Arlington, TX

GOLIATH
235 FT/72 M
Six Flags Magic Mountain, Valencia, CA

THE LONGEST ROLLER COASTERS IN THE UNITED STATES

LENGTH IN FEET

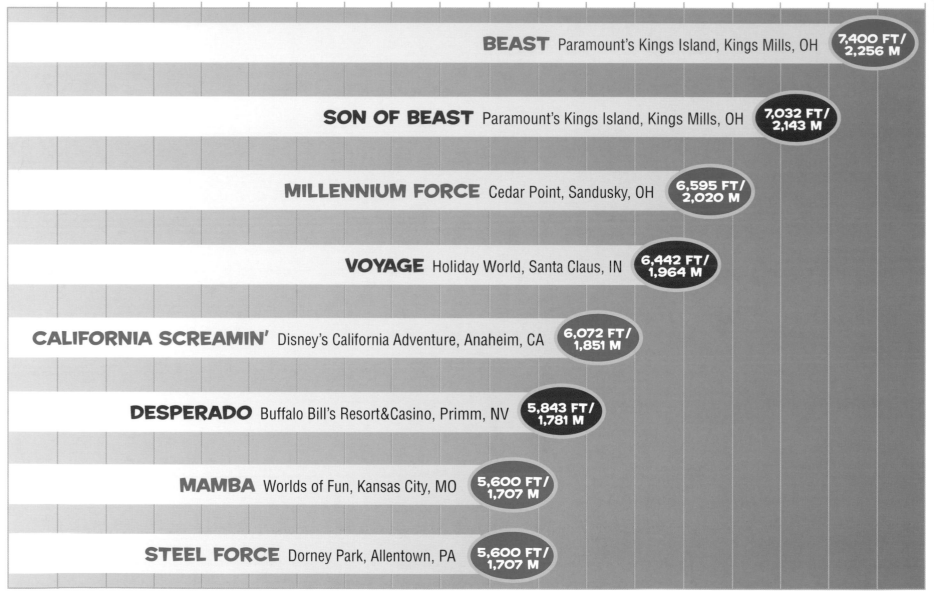

3000	3250	3500	3750	4000	4250	4500	4750	5000	5250	5500	5750	6000	6250	6500	6750	7000	7250	7500

BEAST Paramount's Kings Island, Kings Mills, OH — 7,400 FT/ 2,256 M

SON OF BEAST Paramount's Kings Island, Kings Mills, OH — 7,032 FT/ 2,143 M

MILLENNIUM FORCE Cedar Point, Sandusky, OH — 6,595 FT/ 2,020 M

VOYAGE Holiday World, Santa Claus, IN — 6,442 FT/ 1,964 M

CALIFORNIA SCREAMIN' Disney's California Adventure, Anaheim, CA — 6,072 FT/ 1,851 M

DESPERADO Buffalo Bill's Resort&Casino, Primm, NV — 5,843 FT/ 1,781 M

MAMBA Worlds of Fun, Kansas City, MO — 5,600 FT/ 1,707 M

STEEL FORCE Dorney Park, Allentown, PA — 5,600 FT/ 1,707 M

GLOSSARY

flying coaster a coaster in which the passengers ride while lying down, at times flying forward like Superman

free-fall a coaster in which the passengers drop straight down

G-force gravitational force on riders caused by the rapid acceleration of the coaster

gigacoaster a coaster with a drop or hill 300 feet (91m) or more high

hypercoaster a coaster that has a drop or hill 200 feet (61m) or more high

inverted coaster a coaster that runs beneath the track with its seats attached to the wheel carriage, allowing riders' legs to dangle

lift hill the first and highest hill of a coaster track

LIM linear induction motor that uses magnetic force to pull a coaster through a track

LSM linear synchronous motor that uses high-powered magnets to move a coaster through a track

out-and-back a coaster track that goes out from the station, turns, and comes back

reverse free-fall a coaster in which the passengers drop backward straight down

shuttle coaster a coaster that goes in one direction on the track, stops, and repeats the course again in the opposite direction

stand-up a type of coaster in which the passengers stand up, rather than sit down

steel a type of coaster in which the tracks are made of steel

twister a coaster with a track that winds around itself in all directions

woodie a type of coaster in which the tracks are made of wood

INDEX